# CATCH a DREAMER

Dedicated to
the world of children,
and to those who are
helping make that world
a better place for them

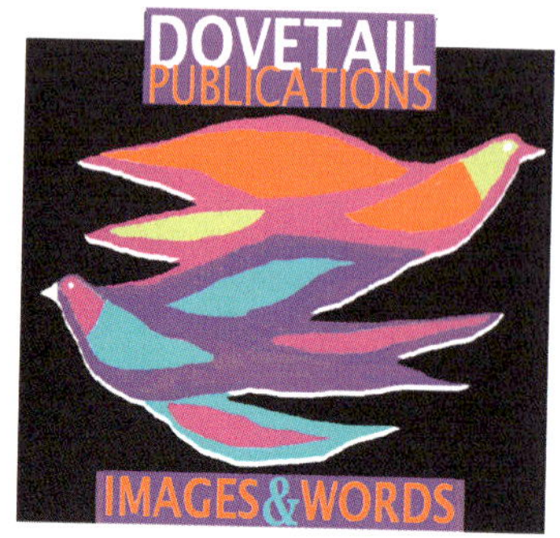




CATCH A DREAMER



Library of Congress Control Number: 2009906893
ISBN-10: 0-615-30524-5
ISBN-13: 978-0-615-30524-0
Printed in the United States

The interior paper stock of this book is supplied by an FSC certified provider
(The mission of the Forest Stewardship Council is to support environmentally appropriate, socially beneficial, and economically viable management of the world's forests).

This book was inspired by the United Nations Declaration of the Ten Rights of The Child

Helen Webber interpreted the United Nations Declaration in a suite of ten tapestries, which became the basis for the art in this book. The words by Jim Petersen are a poetic translation of these rights.

# THE TEN RIGHTS OF THE CHILD

**1 CATCH A DREAMER**
The right to be cherished and protected

**2 LOVE ENFOLDS ME**
The right to affection, love and understanding

**3 I CHASE THE RAIN**
The right to enjoy life without neglect, cruelty and exploitation

**4 DANCE WITH ME**
The right to the best nutrition and medical care

**5 I TALK WITH THE CLOUDS**
The right to special care if physically or mentally challenged

## Inspired by the United Nations Declaration of the Rights of the Child

**6 THE EARTH IS MY MOTHER**
The right to a name and to a place in a nation that cares

**7 WONDER IS REBORN**
The right to be a useful member of society and to develop special abilities

**8 THIS GARDEN IS ALL NEW**
The right to a free education for all children

**9 I DREAM A PARADE**
The right to live in a world of peace and universal brotherhood

**10 WE SHALL SOAR**
The right to enjoy these rights regardless of race, gender, national or social origin

DREAMER

Throw wide
your windows
to the doves,

that carry promise
of a new earth.

Listen to the child within you,

to the dreamer
no one else can hear.

CATCH a DREAMER,
CATCH The DREAM
Helen Webber

Every child has the right to be cherished and protected

LOVE

Hold on to
the ribbons of love...

...ribbons
that will tug the heart
to safe harbor

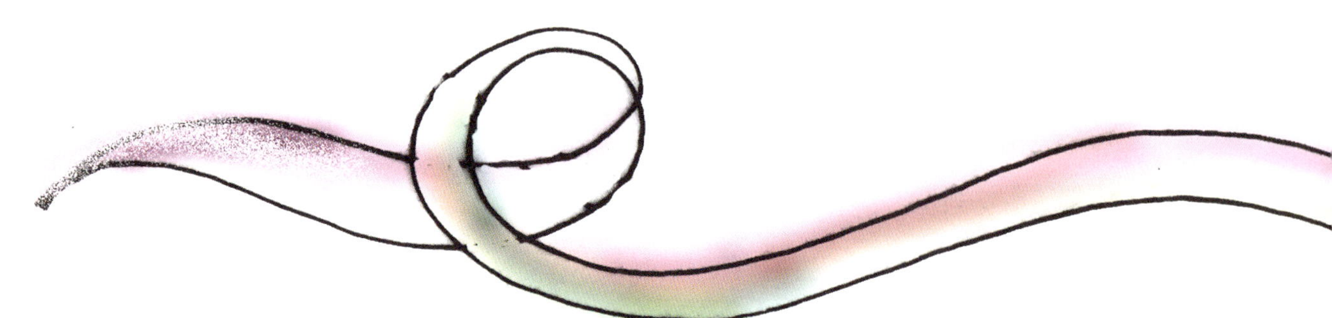

When
Love
enfolds
me
what
shall
I
fear?
Helen Webber

Every child has the right
to affection, love
and understanding

When rain colors your world gray...
RAIN
RAIN

...expect a
RAINBOW!
PLAY

I Chase the RAIN
I PLAY with RAINBOWS

Every child has the right to enjoy life, without neglect, cruelty or exploitation.

When happiness makes you just want to leap, then...

DANCE
DANCE
DANCE

SKIP

SKIP
SKIP
SKIP
Announce yourself with a joyful noise!

DANCE WITh ME SUNLIGHT

Every child has the right to the best nutrition and medical care.

FIND ME

Who can look down
from their sky high perch,
and not count the helping hands,
like leaves in a tree?

FIND ME
A HILLTOP
I'LL TALK
WITH The
CLOUDS
Helen Webber

Every child has the right to special care if physically or mentally challenged.

I share the Earth
with all its
living creatures
and there is
a special place
where I belong

# WHISPERS

Ask the trees,
ask the leaves,
ask the wind.

They know.

The EARTH IS
MY MOTHER
She Whispers
MY NAME
In The WIND
Helen Webber

Every Child has the right to a name and to a place in a nation that cares

My song is
young as the
moon

And old
as the sun

LISTEN
LISTEN
Restless
as water

And open
to wonder

WONDER
IS
REBORN
WITH ME,
LISTEN
Helen Webber

Every child has the right to be a useful member of society and to develop special abilities.

Seed
Let children be given the keys to the garden gate

that they
may grow,
as flowers
grow,
well tended

This
Garden
is all
new
to us.
Here,
the
future
swells
in a
seed
Helen Webber

Every child
has the right
to a free
education

Look beyond
the storm

Proclaim a fresh vision...

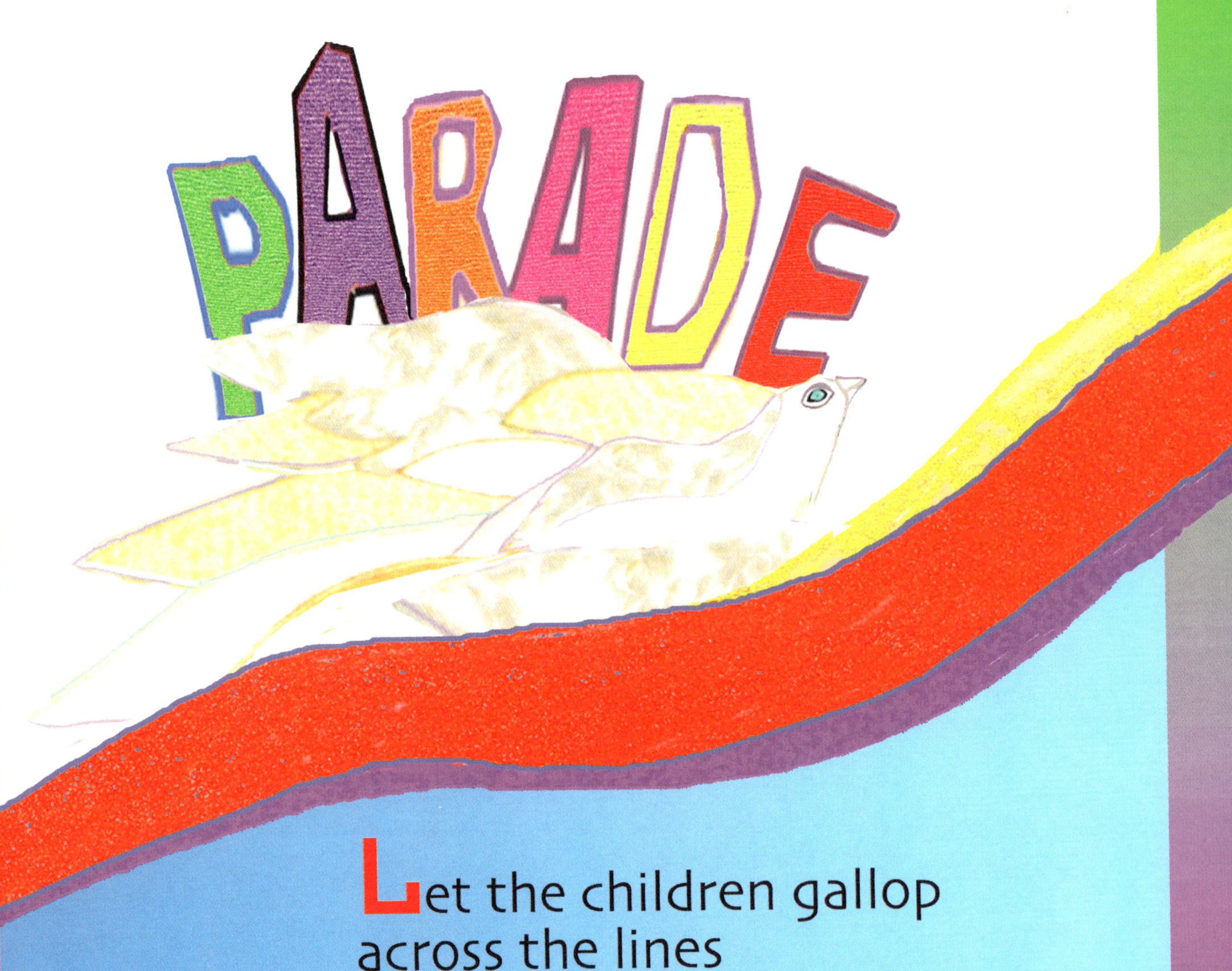


Let the children gallop
across the lines
their parents drew
upon the land

I DREAM a PARADE
PAST ALL FRONTIERS.
NO STORM
TO TURN
US
BACK

Every child has the right
to live in a world of peace
and universal brotherhood

Why did we come here,

and fly this great distance,

if not to surprise you
with our vision
of earth renewed.

WE SHALL
OF MANY COLORED

SOAR ON WINGS,
FEATHERS

Every child,
of every color,
of every creed,
of every nation
and of every
background...

DREAM
PLAY
SOAR
WhisPeR
MY NAME
SKIP
DANCE
ChaSE
LOVE
FIND ME
WONDeR
TALK
LiSTEN
...every child,
girl or boy,
has the right
to enjoy
all of these
rights

## ONCE UPON A TIME A LONG TIME AGO

grown-ups noticed
that the children
could sing in clear voices
and draw original pictures,
could ask important questions,
and speak the truth.
So the grown-ups
bestowed upon the children
the right to help be
guardians of the Earth.

What a time it was then,
when the children ran freely
through the halls
and in the fields.
It was a field day
for laughter
and long stories
told past bed-time.
There was no special time for bed,
only time to do what
made the earth
and its inhabitants flourish.

Why did it all end?
And how?
No one knows for sure,
but the children's right
to share the earth's wonders
was forgotten.
So were many of the children
and their dreams.
Forgotten.

## NOW WE KNOW THE TIME HAS COME

for golden days
and starry nights,
for poems to fill the skies
like fire-flies
and to hear the voices
of the children
rising up through the hills
and in the streets,
of everywhere
reminding us that
now is the time
for the earth's children
to sing their songs,
dance their dances,
and ask important questions.

Helen Webber

THERE IS ONLY ONE CHILD IN the WORLD AND The CHILD'S NAME iS

# ALL CHILDREN

Carl Sandburg

The sale of this book will benefit selected charitable organizations committed to enhancing the lives of children.

For information about the CATCH A DREAMER poster series contact www.dovetailpublications.com

Made in the USA
Charleston, SC
27 January 2013